Kitchen-Tested
ELL Games and Activities

by

Mary Engel

Introduction for ELL and Volunteer Teachers and Aides

by Mary R. Engel, retired ELL teacher

I was privileged to work with adult refugees and other immigrants in teaching English as a second language for more than eight years. I first wrote this book in 1999, but it is being officially published for the first time now.

As individuals struggled to learn English as their second or fourth or fifth language, I worked to create games and activities that would help their efforts be more productive and enjoyable. Every game and activity in this book has been "kitchen-tested" with my students. Along with needed preparation, instructions, and student level, I have included activities, notes, mistakes and lessons learned. The following symbols are used throughout for quick reference.

	Games and Exercises	**Student**	Approximate level of English proficiency
Notes	Suggestions to help an ELL teacher	**Preparation**	Materials needed for the activities
WARNING!	Mistakes I made or lessons I learned	**Instructions**	Details on using the activity.

I divided the games and activities into those for beginning, high beginning, low intermediate, and advanced students. Due to a shortage of teachers in my school, there were only three classes: beginning, intermediate, and advanced. Often the latter two designations were more euphemistic than accurate. Dividing students into groups according to their level of English proficiency is an arbitrary and imperfect procedure but, in my opinion, is preferable to a large multilevel class. However, at times, I have written suggestions for multi-level classes.

Mary Engel
Bismarck, North Dakota

Kitchen-tested
ELL Games and Activities
Table of Contents

ACTIVITIES FOR BEGINNERS

QUESTIONS

Those new to the United States must learn to deal with many questions. The activities here start with the basics. There are questions a newcomer to the United States must learn to answer immediately:
- What's your name (first/last)?
- How do you spell your name?
- What's your address/phone number/Social Security number?

Student

Newcomers

Preparation

Put the individual words from the questions you use on separate slips of paper for students to use. Other questions often asked newcomers in conversation or on an application are:
- Where are you from?
- What is your birth date? Or When is your birthday?
- Are you married or single?
- How many children do you have?
- Do you like (name of city)? Why? Why not?

Instructions

First, practice the questions orally in class.
Next, mix up the slips with words from each question. Give each student a set of question slips with one word on each slip. Have each student put the words in the right order in question form. For example: What/is/your/telephone/number?

Then have each ask a question to another student or to all other students.

Student

Not So Beginning

Make the questions a bit more difficult. For example: What time do you get up/go to bed? What time is it now? When/how do you come to school?

Notes

I see two advantages to this type of activity:
- It helps students understand word order in questions
- It gets the students talking.

Students with even a very limited understanding of our language enjoy asking and answering questions about themselves and their classmates without the teacher as camp director.

A sense of humor knows no language borders. A 22-year-old Iraqi student when asked the question, "Are you married or single?" answered with a twinkle in his eye, "Single with 12 children."

It is important to keep in mind the extent of your students' vocabulary and their ability to use different verb tenses. For example, a very commonly asked question of newcomers is "How long have you been here?" You can help students to respond to that question long before they have the faintest idea of the present perfect tense. Ask the question in class and then paraphrase it. "How long in United States?" or, if you get a blank stare, "When come to United States?" Hopefully, you'll get a month or even a date. Then using a calendar show the student how many weeks or months s/he has been here. Ask the questions again as s/he will hear it, not in pidgin English, until s/he becomes comfortable with answering "two weeks" or whatever the time length is.

REPETITION

Student

Beginning

Repetition is the bedrock of all language learning. Beginning students do not like surprises. Therefore, after studying the present, future, and past tenses, including the most common irregular verbs, I would ask every Friday, "What will you do this weekend?" and every Monday, "What did you do last weekend?"

I thought the students would get as bored with answering as I was in asking the same questions week after week, but I discovered they looked forward to the questions and had their answers ready as soon as I opened my mouth. They were happy to be able to respond with confidence.

CARDINAL/ORDINAL NUMBERS

Student

Beginning

Preparation

Make cards with ordinal numbers, 1st - 31st, and written cardinal numbers, one to thirty-one.

Instructions

Pass out all the ordinal number cards. Then spread out on a table all the cardinal number cards. Have students take turns matching a written cardinal number card with its appropriate ordinal number card. The student with the highest number of matched cards wins.

When I first began working with adults in ELL, I was adamant that they learn the use of ordinal numbers as soon as possible. In working with the calendar, a student had to give the date with an ordinal number. But I finally realized that giving the date as June 2 is as easily understood by Americans as is June 2nd.

However, problems arise if an immigrant lives on a numbered street or in an apartment building. The comment "I live on 4 Street in an apartment on the 3 floor" informs the world that individual knows very little English.

SUPERMARKET ACTIVITIES: FOODS AND SECTIONS

FOODS

Beginning

Prepare cards with names of food and non-food items purchased at a supermarket.

Sample Items:

Pizza	Light Bulbs
Green peppers	Hamburger
Styrofoam cups	Toilet paper
Carrots	Oranges
Trash sacks	Margarine
Paper towels	Ice cream
Bread	Napkins
Milk	Celery
Soap	Eggs
Aluminum foil	Fish
Detergent	

After studying food words and other items found in a supermarket, put the following sections of a supermarket on the board:
- Bakery
- Produce
- Deli
- Dairy
- Paper Products
- Household
- Frozen Foods
- Pet Foods

Instructions

Give each student a card with the name of a food and non-food item purchased at a supermarket. Have each tell you in which section that item would be found.

AT THE SUPERMARKET

Preparation

Prepare a sheet of paper with the names of several food and non-food items. Make a copy for each student.

Instructions

Take a trip to a supermarket. Have students gather at a central location in the supermarket and compare information. Give each student a page, along with the assignment to find the item in the store and to write down the:
- Section in which the item was found
- Brand name of the item, if applicable
- Price

This activity works only with a small group of students, especially if you plan to transport them yourself.

ACTING OUT GAMES

To the Chinese proverb, "A picture is worth a thousand words," can be added, "and a physical demonstration is worth ten thousand words." All of the following acting-out games are noncompetitive. No winners, no losers. I found them useful and fun at the end of a class session for the students to become involved physically in the class and to demonstrate their understanding of previously studied vocabulary.

COMMANDS

Student

Beginning or Intermediate

Preparation

Prepare Command cards

Sample Commands for Beginning Students:
Run around the room.
Take off your shoes.
Stand behind the teacher.
Stand up and sit down.
Close your eyes and go to sleep.
Write your last name on the board.

Turn off the lights, turn on the lights.
Pick up your notebook and put it under your chair.
Pick up your pencil and put it on your head.
Stand on your pencil.
Walk around the room.
Write your first name on the board.
Open the door; close the door.
Clap your hands.
Raise your right arm.
Smile.
Frown.

Sample Commands for Beginning-Intermediate Students:
Shake hands with the student on your right.
Crawl under the table.
Kneel on the floor.
Throw a pencil in the air and catch it.
Scratch your left elbow.
Hiccup and say, "Excuse me."
Motion "Come here" with your hand.
Shake your head.
Clap your hands.
Stand on a chair and jump off.
Scratch your nose.
Throw a pencil in the air and miss it.
Pat your neighbor on the back.
Yawn and say, "Excuse me."
Wave goodbye.
Motion "Go away" with your hand.
Nod your head.

Instructions

Give a command card to each student. Make sure each student understands the command on their card. Have students take turns acting out their commands and the others guess what the action is.

Before you play this game, students must know the verbs used on the command cards.

In playing games with commands, you can introduce social occasions where such actions are appropriate or inappropriate. Point out that in our culture after a yawn, burp, or hiccup, we say "Excuse me" and that nodding your head means "yes," and shaking your head means "no." The same is not true in all cultures.

You may find that students only guess the verb. For example, the command "Run around the room." students may guess "run" and "room" but not "around." Give hints or more information to help out. Demonstrate or illustrate any new words. If this game is played in a class with mixed levels of ability, give the more difficult ones to the advanced students.

GUESS THE ADVERB

In this game all adverbs end in -ly. It is obvious that before you play the game, students must understand what an adverb does in a sentence.

Student

Low to High Intermediate

Preparation

Create cards with a command plus an adverb.
Sample commands:
    Walk around the room *quickly.*
    Offer a chair to a student *politely*.
    Shake hands with a student *happily/gladly*.
    Write your name on the board *carelessly.*
    Say goodbye to a friend *sadly*.
    Walk *slowly* to the door.
    Talk *loudly*.
    Close the door *angrily.*
    Drive around the room *recklessly*.
    Offer a chair to a student *rudely*.
    Write your name on the board *carefully.*
    Open the door *noisily.*
    Open the door *silently.*
    Talk *quietly.*
    Tell something about your country *proudly*.

Instructions

Place cards face down on the table and have each student draw a card. Make sure s/he understands the command.

Ask the other students to guess HOW s/he is carrying out the command. In other words, they do not have to name the action, rather they say HOW it is being acted out.

GUESS THE ADJECTIVE

One night when we played this game with the advanced class, the volunteer teacher for the beginning class failed to show up. Therefore, in the advanced class there were several non-English speaking Ukrainians who didn't understand a single word but could relate to the emotions demonstrated.

Student

Preparation

Intermediate-Advanced

Provide sentence cards and small blank slips of paper.

Sample Sentences:
1. Excuse me, could you tell me where the rest rooms are?

2. My new car cost $10,000.

3. I have a very bad headache.

4. I think you are stupid.

5. Today I am very sad.

6. I am sick because I ate twelve hamburgers and six hot dogs.

7. I had a fight with my boyfriend/girlfriend last night.

8. Excuse me, could you tell me what time it is?

9. I don't want to go to school tonight.

10. Please pass the salt and pepper.

Instructions

Ask students to give you words that tell how a person feels. Write them on the board.
- Have one or two students write the words on small slips of paper.
- Make sure all students understand the emotions to be used.
- Demonstrate any new emotion.
- Hand out sentence cards and have each student pick a slip of paper with an emotion on it.
- Have students take turns reading the sentence card in a way that demonstrates the emotion, regardless of the actual sentence.
- Ask the other students to guess the emotion expressed.

Notes

Adjectives offered by students:
angry happy sad tired nervous scared bored excited worried

Other possible adjectives:
hesitant proud sorry eager confident shy romantic hopeful

GAMES WITH A DECK OF CARDS

LINKING COMMANDS TO A CARD SUIT

Student

Beginning

Preparation

You will need a deck of cards and a blackboard/whiteboard.

Instructions

1. Show the students a deck of cards and give the names of the four suits - spades, hearts, diamonds and clubs. Put the name and symbol for each suit on the board and practice pronouncing the names.

2. Write the following instructions on the board. If you get a:
   ♠ Spade, ask another student a question.
   ♥ Heart, go to the board and write your name.
   ♣ Club, introduce yourself to the person on your right.
   ♦ Diamond, do nothing.

3. Have a student shuffle the deck. (I ask for a volunteer) and pass out one card to each student.

4. The student follows the instruction on the board for his suit.

5. Continue to pass out one card to each student for as long as you wish to play the game. I've found that a total of two or three cards per student is enough for one game. You can also change the instructions for each suit during the game for variety.

Student

Intermediate

Preparation

You will need a deck of cards, a blackboard/whiteboard and Command cards. Although a few of the commands are quite personal, they have never caused any embarrassment for the students, only good-natured laughter.

Create sample Command Cards:
  Ask a student to lend you $10.
  Hiccup.
  Tell the class "I love you" in your language.
  Tell what you would do if you won $1,000,000.
  Pat your head and rub your stomach at the same time.
  Tell what you like and don't like about (name of city).
  Kiss the hand of the student on your left.
  Count from 1 to 20 backwards.
  Stand up and fall down.
  Ask a student for his phone number.
  Crawl around the table.
  Apologize to a student.
  Sit on the teacher's lap.
  Stand on a chair and jump off.
  Say something nice to the person on your left.
  Go to sleep and snore.
  Whisper "I love you" to the person on your right.
  Invite a student to your house to dinner.

Instructions

1. Show the students a deck of cards and make sure they know the names and symbols for all four suits.

2. Write the following instructions on the board: If you draw a:
   ♠ Spade, ask another student a question.
   ♥ Heart, draw a command card and do it.
   ♣ Club, ask the teacher or a student to draw a command card, and you do it.
   ♦ Diamond, do nothing.

3. Have a student shuffle the deck and put it on the table face down. Put command cards face down on the table.

4. One at a time students draw from the deck and respond according to the suit drawn.

Notes

As in the game for beginning students, continue the game as long as you wish. You will notice when interest begins to wane. There are many different commands possible, but I have found reserving one suit for doing nothing adds to the interest. Everyone prays for a diamond.

Advanced

This game takes more time than the previous ones. How long you play depends on interest and time. The game drags if the student asking a question takes too much time deciding who to call on. If this happens, you choose the respondent.

1. Show the students a deck of cards and make sure they know the names and symbols for all four suits.

2. Write the following instructions on the board: If you draw a:
   ♠ Spade, ask another student a question in the past tense.
   ♥ Heart, draw a command card and do it.
   ♣ Club, draw a command card and tell another student or the teacher to do it.
   ♦ Diamond, ask another student a question in the future tense, or another tense the class has studied.

3. Have a student shuffle the deck and put it on the table face down. Put command cards face down on the table.

4. One at a time, have students draw a card and respond according to the suit drawn.

VOWEL SOUND GAMES

MATCHING VOWEL SOUNDS - FRONT VOWELS

Intermediate - Advanced

For the following vowel sound games, show the students how to make the front and back vowel sounds in American English. Demonstrate for each student the position of the tongue and lips. For example, for the sound of the letter A in *and*, the tongue touches the back of the lower teeth and the lips are more open than for other front vowel sounds. Then have each student demonstrate the sound by repeating after you several sample words: and, at, pat, sack.

Many students are able to use a phonetic transcription, but they don't all use the same one. Therefore, where possible, simplify. For example, use the transcription ā for the phonetic symbol [e] as in "ate." The transcriptions for long and short vowel sounds are often used in dictionaries.

Front Vowel Sounds

Symbols and Guide Words:

[I] or ĭ	[i] or ē	[e] or ā	[3] or ĕ	[æ] or ă
s<u>i</u>t	m<u>ee</u>t	st<u>ea</u>k	s<u>ai</u>d	<u>a</u>nd

Minimal pairs are a standby of ELL teaching to help students distinguish between similar vowel sounds. For example, many students cannot hear the difference between "grin" and "green." It's a good idea to practice the front vowel sounds before you play a game using them.

Examples:	[I]	[i]	[e]	[3]	[æ]
	bit	beat	age	bet	bat
	sit	seat	rake	set	sat
	pick	peek	braid	peck	pack
	rid	read	paste	said	sad
	hid	heed	fail	head	had
	did	deed	trace	dead	dad
	grin	green	mail	led	lad

MATCHING VOWEL SOUNDS - BACK VOWELS

Preparation

Make two sets of small cards, one set for each team. Use different colored markers for each set. Put the symbols and guide words listed on the board, and have students practice listening and repeating the sounds.

Instructions

Divide the class into two teams and give each team a set of cards. Have each team lay out its set of cards and match all words with the same vowel sound. There will be five piles, one for each of the five front vowels listed on the board. Make sure the teams are far enough apart so they cannot hear one another easily. The team that correctly matches the two sets of cards first wins the game.

[I] or ĭ	[i] or ē	[e] or ā	[æ] or ĕ	[£] or ă
s<u>ie</u>ve	pl<u>ea</u>se	<u>ai</u>d	s<u>ai</u>d	pl<u>ai</u>d
dam<u>a</u>ge	bel<u>ie</u>ve	w<u>ei</u>gh	br<u>ea</u>d	pr<u>ay</u>er
s<u>i</u>nce	<u>e</u>qual	gr<u>ea</u>t	<u>e</u>very	n<u>a</u>pkin
w<u>o</u>men	rep<u>ea</u>t	g<u>au</u>ge	th<u>e</u>m	c<u>a</u>tch
bic<u>y</u>cle	k<u>ey</u>	v<u>ei</u>l	m<u>ea</u>nt	ma'<u>a</u>m
l<u>i</u>ve	n<u>ie</u>ce	<u>a</u>ncient	<u>e</u>gg	<u>a</u>nimal

Use the same colored marker for all words in each set. Underline all vowel sounds to be matched.

Back Vowel Sounds
Symbols and guide words:

[u]	[ʊ]	[o]	[ɔ]	[a]
glue	took	old	frog	father

Students usually hear the difference between the double o in "cool" and "book" and have no problems with closed o in "old," but they do have problems with the open o [ɔ] in "dog" and the [a] sound of "hot." In some parts of the United States there is no difference in sound between the open o and broad a. Tell your students about regional differences in pronunciation. To me, it's no big deal if the open o is pronounced as a broad a, but you will have language purists in your class who will insist on learning the difference between them.

Preparation

Make two sets of small cards, one set for each team. Use different colored markers for each set.

Put the symbols and guide words for back vowels above on the board and have students repeat the sounds after you.

Instructions

Divide the class into two teams and give each team a set of cards. Have each team lay out its set of cards and match all words with the same vowel sound. There will be five piles, one for each of the five back vowels listed on the board. The team that correctly matches the two sets of cards first wins the game.

[u]	[ʊ]	[o]	[ɔ]	[a]
moon	look	soap	caught	lock
spoon	pull	sold	walk	sergeant
tune	woman	Olympic	log	bomb
soup	full	home	dawn	calm
too	could	soul	gone	heart
blew	wood	open	boss	off
true	sure	toe	cough	operate
smooth	wool	sew	thaw	cop
two	should	low	bought	father
through	put	ocean	autumn	shock

WARNING!

Use the same colored marker for all words in each set. Underline all vowel sounds to be matched.

Notes

There are fifty words in each of the previous two games. To make the game simpler and faster, cut the lists in half.

INDIVIDUAL PRACTICE

Preparation

Create a sheet of paper for each student with guide words numbered 1 - 5 across the top of the paper and all sample words, mixed up, listed in a column underneath. Use the same list of words as in Game Two. You may want to cut the list in half. Underline all vowel sounds to be matched.

Instructions

Have students individually number the words to correspond to the guide words as a 1, 2, 3, 4, or 5.

Individual games take a good deal more time, but they have the advantage of each student struggling by himself and not relying on the more aggressive or advanced student.

Allow at least ten to fifteen minutes for the students to work individually. Then ask for a volunteer to write his words on the board under the appropriate symbols. Other students may disagree. You are the final arbiter. All students who have the words in the correct columns are winners.

DIPHTHONGS

Symbols and guide words:

[ai]	[ou]	[oi]
right	pound	boy

Preparation

Create two sets of small cards, one set for each team as in Games One and Two, or a sheet of paper for each student as in Game Three.

[ai]	[ou]	[oi]
I	hour	toy
eye	out	point
write	noun	voice
quite	town	boil
buy	mouth	joy
ride	house	noise
why	brown	coin
night	loud	oyster
sign	flour	appointment
iron	flower	destroy

Instructions

Play the game and determine the winning team as in Games One and Two.

THE MIDDLE SOUND: UH

This sound, called the schwa, has a symbol which many students know as [ə] or the upside down e. This is the most common vowel sound in spoken American English, and one which drives students crazy if their language has pure vowel sounds.

You can tell your students that in words of three parts or syllables, and in some two part words, the vowel in one of the parts will have an uh sound. Unfortunately, there are one part words with the uh sound, also.

Practice words with the uh sound. A small example of this ubiquitous sound includes:
of, above, even, problem, accident, separate (as a verb), young, was, mountain, region, unusual, student, hundred, some, the, mother

I have included the [ə] sound in the following games that incorporate all the vowel sounds.

GAMES INCORPORATING ALL THE VOWEL SOUNDS

You can play any of the vowel sound games with two teams or as individual competition.

I have found students take comfort playing as a team because vowel sounds are very difficult for most students, and they hesitate to stand alone in their decisions.

Student

High Beginning - Advanced

GAME ONE

Preparation

Create cards for each vowel sound (there will be fourteen guide cards) and small cards with sample words for each sound.

The material below is for either Game One or Game Two. As you lay out the guide cards, mix them up. You don't want all front vowel guide words, for example, together in a row. I've used the guide word, student, to represent the middle sound of uh.

Underline all vowel sounds to be matched. Underline only one vowel sound in each guide and sample word. Do not have more than ten sample words for advanced students or more than five for lower level students.

GUIDE WORDS

s<u>i</u>t c<u>oo</u>l b<u>oo</u>k stud<u>e</u>nt b<u>oy</u> st<u>ea</u>k s<u>ai</u>d p<u>ou</u>nd <u>o</u>ld d<u>o</u>g r<u>i</u>ght h<u>o</u>t m<u>ee</u>t <u>a</u>nd

SAMPLE WORDS

gr<u>ee</u>n	m<u>e</u>t	f<u>a</u>ther	gr<u>i</u>n	p<u>u</u>ll	s<u>igh</u>t	t<u>oy</u>
d<u>a</u>d	t<u>oo</u>	t<u>oe</u>	gr<u>ea</u>t	<u>o</u>f	w<u>o</u>men	w<u>o</u>man
g<u>o</u>ne	h<u>ou</u>se	c<u>a</u>tch	n<u>ie</u>ce	w<u>oo</u>l	sh<u>o</u>ck	<u>a</u>nimal
fr<u>i</u>end	<u>a</u>bove	<u>eye</u>	fl<u>ou</u>r	c<u>o</u>p	g<u>ue</u>st	c<u>a</u>shier
c<u>ou</u>ld	bel<u>ie</u>ve	p<u>a</u>n	m<u>oo</u>n	w<u>oo</u>d	<u>e</u>ven	kn<u>ee</u>
k<u>ey</u>	<u>au</u>tumn	<u>o</u>cean	s<u>i</u>gn	<u>a</u>ncient	qu<u>i</u>t	rep<u>ea</u>t
thr<u>ou</u>gh	th<u>ou</u>gh	b<u>o</u>mb	r<u>e</u>gion	w<u>a</u>s	n<u>a</u>pkin	c<u>oi</u>n
h<u>o</u>me	destr<u>oy</u>	d<u>e</u>bt	s<u>e</u>rgeant	<u>ai</u>d	h<u>ea</u>rt	h<u>ea</u>t
b<u>ou</u>ght	wh<u>y</u>	sh<u>ou</u>ld	tr<u>ai</u>n	pr<u>ay</u>er	un<u>u</u>sual	s<u>oa</u>p
l<u>o</u>g	<u>i</u>ron	s<u>i</u>nce	tr<u>ue</u>	c<u>ou</u>gh	t<u>ow</u>n	<u>oy</u>ster
tw<u>o</u>	b<u>o</u>ss	w<u>eigh</u>	h<u>e</u>lp	m<u>ou</u>th	j<u>oy</u>	s<u>ie</u>ve
l<u>ou</u>sy	th<u>e</u>	<u>e</u>qual	m<u>y</u>th	c<u>a</u>lm	d<u>ow</u>n	s<u>u</u>ch

WARNING! It is extremely important that students have a chance to ask the pronunciation and/or meaning of any word before you begin a game of sounds.

Instructions Spread out the guide cards face up on the table. Put sample word cards in a pile face down on the table. Have students take turns drawing a sample word card, pronouncing it, and placing it under the correct guide word. Be sure students practice pronouncing the guide words before playing the game. If the sample word card is placed correctly, the team or individual keeps the card. If not placed correctly, the card is replaced at the bottom of the pile.

GAME TWO

Preparation Use the cards created for Game One.

Instructions Spread out all guide cards face up on the table. Spread out all sample word cards face up on the table. You pronounce a vowel sound. For example, you say [o] and students look for all sample words containing that sound and place them under the correct guide word. Be sure students practice pronouncing the guide words before playing the game. I allow thirty seconds for each sound. At the end of each round, go among the students and count the number of correctly placed cards. Give them credit, and proceed with another vowel sound. The individual with the highest number of correctly placed cards wins.

If you play this as a team game, give a vowel sound to those on one team, and have them place the sample words for that sound under the correct guide card in a thirty second time span. Then count the accurate word placings and give the team credit for the correct ones. Place the incorrect words back on the table, face up, to be used in another round. Then select a different vowel sound and repeat the process with the other team. The team with the most correctly placed cards wins.

For both individual and team games, you can play as many rounds (with a different vowel sound for each round) as you have the time and interest.

WARNING!

Underline all vowel sounds to be matched. This game is very frustrating to students who have a problem differentiating vowel sounds but is rewarding for those who have a good ear for sounds.

THE "R" FACTOR

Because the letter "r" influences the sound of the vowel preceding it, it's helpful to play a game with vowel sounds plus "r" *after* working with vowel sounds not influenced by "r."

Don't bother with phonetic symbols for this game. Ask the students to listen to the "ear" sound in "beard," the "air" sound in "hair," the "or" sound in "for," and the "er" sound in "word."

Student

High Beginning - Intermediate

Preparation

Prepare four cards with guide words to represent each of the sounds listed above. Ten or more sample words for each of the four sounds. Below are words for either Game One or Game Two.

h<u>air</u>	<u>for</u>	b<u>ear</u>d	w<u>or</u>d
pear	door	weary	pearl
wear	horse	we're	hurl
fare	forlorn	steer	verb
very	floor	here	liar

16

swear	George	tear(noun)	worse
where	coarse	weird	worth
tear(verb)	course	beer	bird
merry	correct	pier	worship
stare	four	fear	skirt
harry	ore	near	hurry

GAME ONE

Place guide word cards face up on the table. Mix up the other cards and pass them out to the students. Give them a couple of minutes to look over their words. Have students take turns pronouncing their words aloud and placing them under the correct guide word.

Students who goof keep the incorrectly placed word until their next turn. The first student to place all their cards under the correct guide word wins.

GAME TWO

Place guide word cards face up on the table. Mix up the other cards and pass them out to the students. Ask students to look over their words but NOT to pronounce them aloud. Have all students place their words at the same time under the guide word cards.

Ask for four volunteers to read the sample words placed under the four guide cards. Usually, there are several misplaced words which the students always correct. Because no one knows who placed the words, no one feels dumb. There are no winners or losers in this game because the group is learning as a whole unit.

GAME THREE

Advanced

Put the four guide words, **hair, for, beard,** and **word** on the board and have students take turns writing on the board as many words as possible under each. If students don't want to write on the board, because they're not sure of their spelling, play the game orally. A student gives a word and says under which guide word it should go. If not challenged, the word is accepted. You or a volunteer write the word given orally on the board.

I have played this game as a no winner/no loser game. However, if you appoint a score keeper to keep track of the number of correct placings, the individual with the most correctly placed words would win.

During the times I've played this game orally, I've never had an incorrect placement go undetected. If an incorrect placement should go unchallenged, you, the teacher, would have to speak up.

REGULAR VERBS IN THE PAST

PRONUNCIATION GAMES

The first two games lend themselves to competition, the third does not.

Students will not know the meaning of all the verbs, and this is bothersome to them. Therefore, I explain or demonstrate the meaning of any unknown verb. I disagree with ELL professionals who say that when you're stressing pronunciation, meaning is not important. You can teach meaning with pronunciation and have fewer frustrated students.

Student

Preparation

Beginning

Create small cards with regular verbs in the past. Following are forty regular verbs in the past to get you started. You can think of more examples.

[t]	[d]	[3d]
raced	rained	needed
picked	pulled	seeded
touched	bathed	repeated
talked	cleaned	painted
pronounced	snowed	rented
danced	rowed	planted
jumped	used	added
kicked	dried	decided
washed	died	ended
walked	owed	wanted
slapped	smelled	noted
spanked	smiled	omitted
slipped	weighed	edited
kissed	showed	seated
laughed	played	orated

Review the three possible pronunciations of regular verbs in the past. As students love rules, they greatly appreciate the specific rules that govern the sounds of -ed at the end of regular verbs in the past.

Beginning students tend to pronounce the -ed ending as [3d] for **all** regular verbs.

GAME ONE

Spread out all cards on the table; give students time to look over the cards. Ask if there are any words they want you to pronounce for them.

Have the students take turns picking a card and pronouncing the verb. If correct, the student keeps the card.

GAME TWO

This game has three rounds.

One: Have each student pick up two cards (or more, depending on the number of players) with verbs ending in the sound [t].

Two: Have each pick up two or more cards with verbs ending in the sound [d].

Three: Have each pick up two or more cards with verbs ending in the sound (3d]. Repeat until all cards are gone.

Students keep all verbs correctly pronounced. The student with the most cards wins.

GAME THREE

Put the symbol for each of the three sounds on separate cards.

Have students take turns placing the verb cards under the appropriate symbol card: [t], [d], and [3d].

RHYMING GAMES

MATCHING RHYMING WORDS

Beginning

Create two sets of small cards. Write the rhyming words on each set using different colored markers.

Sample rhyming words:

seem - dream	met - set
say - day	blow - go
pick - stick	said - red
tie - my	new - too
mellow - yellow	hat - sat
night - write	soon - tune
meat - greet	tall - fall
me - tea	green - lean
since - rinse	mile - while
toe - sew	come - hum
ache - make	heard - purred
zoo - glue	late - straight

Put all cards face up on the table. Have students take turns matching the words that rhyme. Or put one set of cards face down on the table and spread out the other set. Have students draw a word card from the pile and match it with a word on the table.

Either way, the student must pronounce both words correctly. The student keeps each pair s/he has matched correctly.

Although many of these pairs seem too obvious, I have found that an easy game boosts beginning students' self-confidence.

Intermediate

Develop four sets of cards using a different colored marker for each set. Sample rhyming sets:

dies	size	buys	wise
tough	rough	enough	stuff
dumb	come	hum	thumb
cent	meant	scent	tent
insist	persist	kissed	mist
sure	lure	tour	boor
loud	crowd	cloud	shroud
ease	sneeze	bees	tease
juice	loose	moose	noose
ocean	motion	lotion	notion
defeat	delete	complete	repeat
weight	bait	gate	wait
early	curly	pearly	surly
news	lose	booze	sues
seize	trees	sees	seas

Using card sets with the rhyming words, place one set face down on the table and spread out the other three sets face up.

Have students take turns drawing a card from the pile face down on the table and finding three other words that rhyme with the word drawn. S/he pronounces the four words and, if correct, keeps the four cards.

If not correct, s/he puts the drawn card at the bottom of the pile and places the other three cards face up on the table.

The winner is the one with the most cards.

Advanced

Students find the second game more challenging. You'll be surprised at the number of words they can think of and at the good-natured correcting of one another. The first game is competitive; the second cooperative.

Make two sets of small cards using a different colored marker for each set. Sample words:

sewed - flowed	flower - hour
mine - sign	chew - due

lake - break	was - does
night - height	weight - late
mean - scene	sneeze - trees
aisle - while	stare - mayor
home - comb	debt - get
some - dumb	whirls - curls
reign - pane	islands - highlands
though - doe	subtle - cuddle
stuff - rough	greet - suite
of - shove	fires - pliers
firm - worm	phone - loan

GAME ONE

Instructions

This game follows the procedures of the previous rhyming games. Spread out both sets of cards, face up, and match the rhyming words, or put one set in a pile and have students draw a card and match with its corresponding word from cards spread on the table. If the student is correct, s/he keeps both cards. If incorrect, s/he must replace the cards.

GAME TWO

Instructions

Use only one set of cards. Place the pile face down on the table. Have students draw one card at a time and come up with as many rhyming words as they can think of.

MATCHING SOUNDS

CONSONANT SOUNDS

Student

Preparation

Students learning English have myriad problems in understanding spoken American English. Many times I've been asked the question in a plaintive voice, "Teacher, what 'didja mean?" And in everyday conversation, the answer to "Howya doin'?' is often "Priddy good." Why don't we pronounce the "b" in "debt" and "s" in "island?" And why do we pronounce the double "t" in "written" as a "t" but the double "t" in "pretty" as a "d"?

After students have become familiar with some of our goofy ways of pronouncing, they like to test their knowledge in a game. For either game, underline the consonant sounds to be matched.

Words for Game One or Game Two:

si<u>z</u>e - ri<u>s</u>en	be<u>tt</u>or - wri<u>tt</u>en	be<u>tt</u>er - bu<u>tt</u>er
e<u>d</u>ucation - sol<u>di</u>er	pla<u>c</u>e - ob<u>sce</u>ne	wi<u>th</u>out - mo<u>th</u>er
<u>s</u>ugar - transmi<u>ss</u>ion	<u>th</u>eater - bo<u>th</u>	<u>s</u>uggest - <u>j</u>am
suspi<u>ci</u>ous - mo<u>ti</u>on	<u>gh</u>ost - <u>g</u>o	enou<u>gh</u> - rou<u>gh</u>
<u>th</u>ough - dou<u>gh</u>	dum<u>b</u> - de<u>bt</u>	<u>sc</u>old - <u>sc</u>our
<u>sc</u>ene - <u>c</u>ent	tea<u>ch</u> - na<u>t</u>ural	pic<u>t</u>ure - men<u>ti</u>on
li<u>f</u>e - geogra<u>ph</u>y	pu<u>sh</u> - o<u>c</u>ean	<u>j</u>elly - loun<u>g</u>e
si<u>gn</u> - whi<u>n</u>e	si<u>ck</u> - <u>C</u>hristmas	<u>h</u>ot - <u>h</u>ome
plea<u>s</u>ure - gara<u>g</u>e	a<u>i</u>sle - sme<u>ll</u>	<u>h</u>onest - <u>h</u>our
<u>g</u>et - <u>g</u>reen	pa<u>g</u>e - <u>j</u>ail	<u>wh</u>o - <u>h</u>ow

Intermediate - Advanced

GAME ONE

Use two sets of small cards with words written in different colored ink.

Place one set face down in a pile and spread out the other set face up. Students take turns drawing a card from the pile and matching it with a card on the table with the same sound.

You can also spread out both sets of cards and have students match words with the same sound. Either way the student with the most cards wins.

GAME TWO

I have only played Game Two with a small group of students. I doubt if it would work with a large group.

Make a sheet of paper for each student with the words in two columns (thoroughly mixed up).

Give each student a copy of the mixed up words. Have students match the consonant sounds. Set a time period of five minutes and then share results. Ask for a volunteer to read his list but encourage others to chime in. The student with the greatest number of matched sounds wins.

In the previous games of matching consonant sounds, it is obvious there are several words with the same sound. For example, you can match the **s** in **sugar** with the **c** in **ocean** or the **t** in **motion**, as well as with the **ss** in **transmission**.

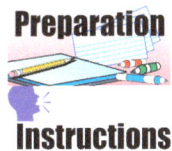

Alert your students to these possibilities or create a game without any duplicate sounds. Personally, I welcome all possible combinations.

VOWEL AND CONSONANT SOUNDS

High Beginning - High Intermediate

After students have become familiar with some of our goofy ways of pronouncing, they like to test their knowledge in a game.

Create two sets of small cards written with different colored markers. Underline the letter/s in each word giving the sound/s you want students to match.

Words for either Game One or Game Two:

so - sew	school - strike	flew - glue
sun - sign	kiss - place	those - doze
sure - shoe	ghost - get	thumb - debt
these - then	think - through	aisle - I'll
jelly - orange	beige - rouge	know - new
telephone - fill	through - threw	walk - calm
either - need	hour - honest	have - hold
hurt - pert	picture - pitcher	rain - feign

GAME ONE

Spread out both sets of cards face up on the table. Ask if there are any words students want pronounced. Then have students take turns matching the underlined sounds. If correct, the student keeps the cards. The student with the greatest number of cards wins.

GAME TWO

Play the game as a Concentration game. Spread out all cards face down on the table. A student turns up two cards at a time, if the sounds match, the student keeps both cards. If the sounds don't match, the cards go back face down, and another student tries. The student with the greatest number of matched cards wins. Allow at least fifteen minutes for this game.

WORKING WITH OPPOSITES AND SYNONYMS

The first pair of opposites I work with is **different** and **same**. There are numerous ways to illustrate their meanings. Use objects in the room: table/chair vs. two identical chairs, pencil/pen vs. two pencils; or use the students: men/women vs. two or three women, students speaking Vietnamese/Russian vs. two or three Russian-speaking students.

In English we have many words that mean the same thing. For example, **under**, **below**, **beneath**, **underneath**. I realize that to language purists there are slight differences in meaning for these words, but I'm happy if my students grasp the general meaning of something that is down lower than something else.

I work with opposites and synonyms alternately; that is, I say these words mean something different or these words mean the same. The neat thing about working with either opposites or synonyms is that most are easy to act out with few or no props. We'll begin with opposites.

UNDERSTANDING OPPOSITES

Student

Beginning

Preparation

Create two sets of small cards with words written in different colors. If there are only a few students in your class, have them work together. If there are six or more students, make two sets of cards with opposite words for each two students and have them work together. I've found at the beginning level, the need to compete with another team is not strong. Each team is concentrating on completing its own task.

One advantage of putting the words on cards is that students can take them home and copy the words in their notebooks with translations in their own language. My students always returned the cards at the next class session. Sample words:

same - different	false - true	south - north
east - west	weak - strong	polite - rude
up - down	early - late	over - under
good - bad	sick - well	on - under
front - back	in - out	short - long
next to - across from	full - empty	short - tall
pretty - ugly	sour - sweet	before - after
in front of - behind	inside - outside	top - bottom

hot - cold	wet - dry	forward - backward
big - little	fast - slow	happy - sad
old - new	old - young	

Instructions

The task is to match the opposite words. You can also manipulate the words above showing **place** by using Cuisenaire rods. This is an exercise in practicing colors as well as **place** opposites. For example, ask a student to pick up a red rod and a black rod. Then tell the student to put the red rod under the black one. I've found by manipulating the rods, the student can better visualize the concepts of **under** or **on** or **next to**, etc.

Or, if you've been teaching numbers to beginning students, make cards from 1 - 20 or by tens from 20 to 100. Ask a student to pick up a 20 and hold it over a 50, for example. If you want to make this a competitive game, then the student who responds with the most correct answers wins. I have not played the game this way because with beginning students I have found that completing a task successfully is the most important goal.

GAME TWO

Student

High Beginning

Preparation

Create two sets of small cards with words in different colors.

quiet - noisy	push - pull	narrow - wide
cheap - expensive	absent - present	question - answer
hard - easy	lose - find	awake - asleep
hard - soft	thick - thin	right - wrong
public - private	fat - thin	far - near
dark - light	heavy - light	first - last
arrive - go/leave	everyone - no one	more - less
rich - poor	clean - dirty	few - many
right - left	low - high	little - much
stop - go	nothing - everything	
come - go/leave	yesterday - today	

Instructions

Place one set of cards face down in a pile and spread out the other set on a table. Have students take turns matching opposites. If correct, the student keeps the pair, if not, s/he replaces both cards, and another student takes a turn. The student with the most correctly matched cards wins.

Of course, you don't introduce *little/much* or *few/many* until you've talked about things you can count and things you cannot count, officially know as Count and Non-Count Nouns.

GAME THREE

Intermediate

Create two sets of cards with words in different colors.

smooth - rough	double - single	together - separate
often - rarely	future - past	remember - forget
tight - loose	sharp - dull	freeze - melt
permanent - temporary	follow - lead	stay - leave
most - least	always - never	best - worst
go to bed - get up	common - unusual	win - lose
succeed - fail	crooked - straight	
wholesale - retail	increase - decrease	
at the top of - at the bottom of		

The procedure for playing and winning is the same as for the previous game.

SYNONYMS

Beginning

The following game is not one to play the first week of school. You can play a simple game of opposites early in the learning process, but don't introduce a synonym game until students have learned enough English to realize there are often one or more words that have the same or similar meaning.

Make two sets of small cards for each team. Use a different colored marker for the first and second words in a set. Sample words:

simple - easy	pretty - beautiful	year - 365 days
leave - go	over - above	wash - clean
good-looking - handsome	month - 4 weeks	under - below
Saturday and Sunday - weekend	week - 7 days	fine - good
so-so - pretty good	after - later	slender - thin
come - arrive	high - tall	thin - skinny
light - lamp	say - tell	speak - talk
right - correct	wrong - incorrect	finish - end

hard - difficult   sad - unhappy   big - large
rapid - fast   small - little   much/many - a lot

Draw stick figure pictures to show the difference between slender, thin, and skinny before you play the game.

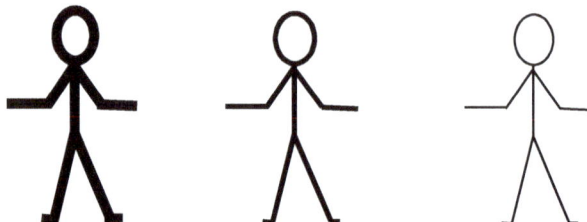

Give each team two sets of cards and have the teams spread out their cards face up. The students in each team take turns matching the synonyms. The team that completes pairing synonyms correctly first wins. You are the judge.

An alternative way to play is to put a set of cards for each team in a pile face down and the other set face up on the table. The students in each team take turns drawing from the pile and matching it with a synonym on the table. The team that completes pairing synonyms correctly wins. You are the judge.

Student

Intermediate

Preparation

The materials and procedure(s) are the same as for the preceding game.

cupboard - cabinet	throw - toss	empty - vacant
look for - search	jump - leap	push - shove
couch - sofa	wide - broad	rarely - seldom
sometimes - occasionally	here - present	gift - present
yell - shout	plump - chubby	start - begin
beside - next to	near - close	quickly - fast
always - forever	return - come back	stay - remain

Variation:
Match two synonyms and one opposite. Most words in the preceding lists lend themselves to an opposite that the students know. For example: simple/easy - hard, empty/vacant - full, throw/toss - catch, after/later - now, fast/rapid - slow, start/begin - stop. You get the idea.

WARNING!

Remember to play games with synonyms *before* you add opposites in the same game.

28

Advanced

The materials and procedure(s) for this game are the same as for beginning and intermediate students. Below are words I've used successfully with advanced students.

lengthen - extend	calm - serene	real - authentic
hurt - injured	shore - beach	drunk - tight
bother - annoy	skip - omit	actual - real
influence - affect	wages - income	danger - risk
convict - prisoner	grab - seize	change - alter
huge - immense	sympathy - empathy	fat - obese
abbreviate - shorten	recess - playtime	nervous - edgy
should - ought to	poor - needy	1' - 1 foot
1 quart - 32 ounces	36" - 1 yard	1" - 1 inch
observe - notice	crooked - dishonest	1 pint - 16 ounces
resident - inhabitant	factory - plant	bag - sack
dare - challenge	effect - result	silly - foolish
sufficient - enough	absurd - ridiculous	adjust - adapt
only - just	imagine - pretend	intend - mean
condition - situation	facilities - conveniences	
participation - involvement		

WARNING!

There are too many words in the list above for one game. Too many words are very frustrating and make a game a chore. I use no more than fifteen pairs in one game because:

1. There will be words that students don't know. For example, involvement. Give other words such as, to be a part of, to be included in.

2. After the game, students want to know what the difference is between actual/real and real/authentic. We also talk about the slight difference in the meanings of sympathy and empathy.

Variations

SYNONYM DEFINITION GAME

This is a game of words and their definitions.

Use two sets of small cards and put words in one color and definitions in another. The student with the most correctly matched cards wins. A small sampling of possible words/definitions follows:

1. remind - cause to remember

2. consult - ask for advice or information

3. dumb - cannot speak

4. illiterate - unable to read or write

5. invulnerable - cannot be hurt or damaged

7. stationery - paper to write letters on

8. stationary - cannot be moved

9. convention - a large meeting that usually lasts two or three days

10. extend - to make longer

11. envelope - what you put a letter in

12. incredible - not believable

13. outer space - beyond Earth's atmosphere

SYNONYMS THROUGH EXAMPLES

Preparation

To reinforce understanding in the preceding synonym game, write sentences on cards illustrating the usage of the words and have students give the correct synonym. Either underline the important words to be replaced with a synonym or leave a blank space to fill in. Below are sample sentences for the synonyms in the preceding list. Play this game one or two class sessions after you've played the synonym definition game.

1. Scientists are studying far away stars, suns, and planets.

2. You made $1,000 yesterday at work!! That's _____.

3. Tall buildings are immovable.

4. After I write a letter, I put it in an _____.

30

5. She bought some <u>pretty blue paper</u> to write letters on.

6. You'll have to <u>make</u> the class <u>longer</u> if we're supposed to learn everything you want us to.

7. Because she <u>cannot speak</u>, she communicates in writing.

8. I'll be in Chicago at our company's <u>big meeting</u>.

9. I have a terrible memory. Please _____ me.

10. Some people seem <u>never to be hurt</u>, regardless of what happens

Instructions

Spread out the cards and let students choose one card at a time and give the word or phrase that means the same as the underlined word(s) or fills in the blank. The student with the most cards wins.

WARNING!

Tell the students that in sentences 7 and 10, they will have to add "is" and "are," respectively.

TWO SYNONYMS AND ONE OPPOSITE

Preparation

Using the preceding lists of synonyms and opposites, make two sets of small cards with all synonyms in the same color and make one set of opposites in a different color.

Instructions

Spread out the synonym cards face up on the table and put the opposite cards in a pile face down. Have students take turns drawing from the pile of opposite cards and matching with two synonym cards. If a student chooses an incorrect synonym, that card goes back on the table face up and the opposite card is put back in the pile of opposite cards. The student with the most correctly matched cards wins.

GAMES WITH PREPOSITIONS

CHOOSING PREPOSITIONS

Prepositions are the bugaboo of learning English (and other languages). I begin with the basic prepositions: **in, at, to, on**, and **between**. After you've explained to them the anomalies of getting <u>on</u> a bus or plane but <u>in</u> a taxi or car, of being born **on** a day or date but **in** a month or year, and living **on** a street but **at** a certain street address, and after doing umpteen exercises showing the various uses of the above prepositions (I haven't even mentioned

why we have two words: **between** and **among** to describe the simple concept of **in the midst of two or three or more**)—then play games.

Beginning

Make sentence cards with blanks for prepositions. Put the prepositions **in, at, to, on, between** on the board.

1. I live _____ Main Street _____ Green and Maple Avenues.

2. What time do you go _____ school?

3. I get up early _____ the morning and go _____ bed _____ midnight.

4. _____ night we watch TV.

5. _____ the evening I study my lesson for school.

6. My friend lives _____ the corner of 5th Street and Avenue C.

7. My family has a big party _____ Christmas time.

8. _____ New Year's Eve we always go _____ a friend's house.

9. Where's your husband? He's _____ work.

10. Where's your wife? She's _____ school.

11. I get _____ the plane _____ Minneapolis _____ 4:30 p.m.

12. They live _____ 43rd Street _____ Chicago.

13. I was born _____ March 18 _____ 1967.

14. I got _____ my bike and rode _____ school.

15. _____ Halloween we go from house _____ house asking for candy.

16. There are not many weeks _____ Thanksgiving and Christmas.

17. We go _____ school _____ Mondays and Fridays _____ the morning.

18. They live _____ Apartment 22 _____ 1500 10th St.

19. It is time to leave. Please get _____ the car.

20. I go _____ work _____ 7:00 a.m.

Place all sentence cards face down on the table. Have students take turns drawing a card, reading it, and stating the correct preposition/s from those on the board. Where there is more than one possible preposition, I have indicated it in the game below. When students answer correctly, they keep the sentence card. If incorrect, replace the sentence card face down on the table. The person who has the most sentence cards wins the game.

Twenty sentence cards may be too many for beginning students. Adjust the number to fit your group.

Variation:
Give each student a sheet with ten to fifteen sentences using the same prepositions as in the previous game. Have each student work individually. Go over the results as a group. The student with the most correct answers wins.

Low to High Intermediate

After you have studied more prepositions, play a game to reinforce learning. Your students need to know which prepositions they are expected to know for whatever preposition game you play. The following prepositions are used in this game: **at, of, about, during, to, by, on, with, in, for, near, between, around, next to, in front of.** Where there is a possibility of more than one preposition, I've listed the possibilities at the end of the game.

For a team game create sentence cards with blanks for prepositions. Place cards in a pile, face down.

For an individual game use a sheet of paper for each student with sentences and blanks for the preposition(s).

1. I'm thinking _____ going to Miami _____ Easter break.

2. I'll take the plane _____ Chicago and then go _____ bus _____ New York.

3. Don't complain _____ your job _____ me. Talk _____ your boss.

4. I love my kids, but I don't approve _____ everything they do.

5. What do you do _____ old plastic sacks you don't want?

6. A big man _____ a tall cowboy hat sat _____ me _____ the movies, and I couldn't see anything.

7. He lives _____ the Missouri River, but I live _____ the east part _____ town.

8. Have you heard _____ the new miracle medicine?

9. I need _____ go _____ the store _____ buy some bread and milk.

10. I need _____ go _____ the store _____ some bread and milk.

11. I'm not interested _____ watching TV tonight.

12. _____ you and me, I think she's crazy.

13. I'm not sure, but I think I'll arrive _____ 5:00 p.m.

14. The post office is _____ the corner _____ the drugstore.

15. What do you think _____ the discussions in Congress _____ the Democrats and Republicans?

1. of, about / during, at	9. to, to, to
2. to, by, to	10. to, to, for
3. about / to or with / to, with	11. in
4. of	12. between
5. with	13. around, about, by
6. with / in, in front / ahead of / at	14. near, on, around / from, near, by
7. near, by, on / in/ of	15. of, between
8. of, about	

Instructions

Team Game: Have a member of one team draw a card, read the sentence aloud, and supply the correct preposition/s. Teammates may help. If the team is correct, it keeps sentence card. If it is wrong, it replaces the card at the bottom of the pile. The team with the most sentence cards wins the game.

Individual Game: Set a time period (for fifteen sentences, allow ten minutes). Check answers as a group. The person with the most correct answers is the winner. There are usually multiple winners.

Give credit to a student who chooses an alternative you haven't listed.

IMPACT OF THE PART OF SPEECH

FUN WITH *OVER*

This activity is not competitive. I've used it with very advanced students at the end of a class session for them to learn the extent of their understanding of idiomatic English. If students work alone, I review the list with each of them. If they work as a group, we look at the list together.

One reason it is important to list the part of speech with each word can be seen with #5. As a noun (as in this activity), it means costs of production, but as an adverb, it simply means a location above an object.

If you teach a multi-level class, you might give some of the over words to your very advanced students to work on while you work with other students. The activity is vocabulary enhancing, I assure you.

Make a list of the *over* words you will use in the activity. For example,

1. overwhelm (v) -
2. overpass (n) -
3. overseas (n) -
4. overhear (v) -
5. overhead (n) -
6. over and above (adv) -
7. oversee (v) -
8. overweight (adj) -
9. overhaul (v, n) -
10. overcharge (v,n) -
11. overall (adj) -
12. overalls (n) -
13. overbearing (adj) -
14. overboard (adv) -
15. overcast (adj) -
16. overcome (v) -
17. overdo (v) -
18. overdraft (n) -
19. overdue (adj) -
20. overkill (v) -
21. overlook (v) -
22. overrule (v) -
23. oversight (n) -
24. overstate (v) -
25. overtake (v) -
26. overdose (v, n) -
27. overthrow (v, n) -
28. overtime (n) -
29. leftover or left-over (adj) -
30. leftovers or left-overs (n) -

Can you guess the meanings of the words above? The basic meanings of over are **above, more than, on the other side of.** To help you guess the meaning of the over words, look at the part of speech for each word. Whichever way you use this activity, it takes a lot of time. The thirty words listed here are too many to use at once.

Do NOT, repeat, do NOT use all thirty words in one game. I did the first time I tried the activity and it was a disaster. Don't use more than ten words at a time.

TWO-PART VERBS

THE UBIQUITOUS GET

Before you play a game, put the more common uses of get + preposition(s) on the board: get up, get in (into), get on, get to, get away, get off, get out of, get over, get away (with), get along (with). This is certainly not an exhaustive list, but it will do for starters.

The two most troubling problems in learning basic English, I think, are prepositions by themselves and verbs plus prepositions which make up so many of our idioms. I stressed prepositions earlier.

Now let's work with common two-part verbs. I always begin with the ubiquitous verb, **get**.

On the board write the basic meanings of the verb get: receive, obtain, achieve, catch, earn. Then illustrate and/or ask for examples from the students for each meaning.
For example:

receive:	I got a letter from my parents last week.
obtain:	He got a new job last week.
achieve:	She got an award for best soccer player.
catch:	I'm afraid my kids are getting a cold,
earn:	How much do you get each week at work?

And that's just for starters. When you add a preposition to get (receive, obtain) a whole new set of problems arises.

High Beginning and Low Intermediate

For Game One, put the correct form of get on the get + preposition cards, so that the student does not have to change the tense of the verb or the person.

1. What time do you _____ work?

2. What time do your kids _____ in the morning to go to school?

3. She _____ the taxi every morning to go to school.

4. We _____ the airplane at 6:00 p.m. yesterday.

5. The robber didn't _____ robbing the bank. The police caught him.

6. They don't always _____. They often argue.

7. I hope to _____ from vacation about August 20th.

8. My son has had a bad cold for a week. He can't _____ it.

9. Why do Americans _____ a bus, but _____ a car?

10. My friend stopped at the corner of 5th St. and Main and I _____ the car.

1. get off	6. get along
2. get up	7. get back
3. gets in	8. get over
4. got on	9. get on, get in
5. get away with	10. got out of

Preparation

Make:
Sentence cards with blank spaces for get + preposition(s).
Small cards with get + preposition(s).

Instructions

Place sentence cards in a pile, face down on the table. Spread out get + preposition cards face up. Have students take turns picking up a sentence card and selecting the appropriate get + preposition card that completes the sentence card.

If a student selects the correct get + preposition card, he keeps it. If not, he places it face up on the table, and another student has a chance to select a get + preposition card to complete the sentence. The other team members may help. The team with the most sentence cards correctly completed wins the game.

GAME TWO

Student

Low Intermediate- High Intermediate

Preparation

Make two sets of cards written in different colored markers -
one set with the definition and the other with the two-part verb.

Definition	Two-part verb
Invite on a date.	Ask out.
Return (something).	Bring back.

Raise children	Bring up
Cause	Bring about.
Machine doesn't work	Break down
Interrupt	Break in
Illegal entry	Break into
Train someone	Break (someone) in
End a romance	Break up
Wear clothes	Have on
Become friends again	Make up
Cancel	Call off
Postpone	Put off
Visit briefly	Drop in/by
Meet accidentally	Run into/across
Get control	Take over
Shorten a piece of clothing	Take up
Resemble	Take after
Appear	Show up

Instructions

Have students take turns matching the definitions with the two-part verbs. The winner is the student(or the team) with the most number of cards correctly matched.

GAME THREE

Student

Low Intermediate- High Intermediate

Preparation

Create sentence cards with blank spaces for get + preposition/s and small cards with get + preposition/s.

1. Some Americans talk so fast, I can't _____ what they're saying.

2. I'll drive tomorrow. What time do you want me to _____ you?

3. You're making too much noise! _____ it _____!

4. He's a terrible man. I don't understand how she can _____ him.

5. The sign says, "No Smoking." Please _____ your cigarette.

6. My kids never _____ their clothes in the closet.

7. If you'll be home tomorrow about 3:00, I'll _____ for a cup of tea.

8. Please _____ the TV. I can't hear it.

9. You must _____ your application to the employment office.

10. My car is old, but I hope it doesn't _____ on my trip to California.

11. Before I buy this used car, I'd like to _____ it _____.

12. Before you buy a pair of shoes, it is important to _____ them _____.

13. I don't know the answer, but I'll _____ for you.

14. She missed three hours of work last week, but she'll _____ them _____ this week.

15. I don't understand my sister and her boyfriend. One week they _____, the next week they _____.

1. figure out or make out	9. turn in or hand in
2. pick up	10. break down
3. cut, out	11. try, out
4. put up with	12. try, on
5. put out	13. find out
6. hang up	14. make, up
7. drop by/in	15. break up, make up
8. turn up	

Instructions

Play this game after your students have studied a number of verbs + prepositions and understand their idiomatic meanings.

Place sentence cards in a pile, face down on the table. Spread out the verb + preposition cards on the table.

If a student selects the correct verb + preposition card, he keeps the sentence card. If not, he places the verb + preposition card face up on the table, and another student takes a turn. The other team members may help. The team with the most sentence cards correctly completed wins the game.

GAME FOUR

Create a sheet of paper for each student with all prepositions used written at the top of the paper with instructions for the student to supply the correct preposition to the verb to equal the definition given.

As this is an individual game, allow time in class to check and/or correct answers. The student with the most correct answers wins.

1. ask _____ = invite someone on a date. (out)

2. bring _____ = raise kids. (up)

3. call _____ = visit or ask to speak in class. (on)

4. call _____ = cancel. (off)

5. call _____ = return a phone call. (back)

6. check _____ = register at a motel. (in/into)

7. check _____ = take a book from the library. (out)

8. check _____ = pay your bill and leave a motel. (out of)

9. do _____ = repeat doing something. (over)

10. drop _____ = informal, short visit. (by/in)

11. drop _____ = leave something/someone at a place. (off)

"LET'S TALK"

Student

Preparation

Intermediate - Advanced

Make slips of paper with questions.

1. Who in your family do you **take after**?

2. For what reason would you **call off** a picnic?

3. What was the last piece of clothing you **tried on** at a store?

4. How would you feel if you gave a party and no one **showed up**?

5. Where do you think is a good place to **bring up** kids?

6. When you're calling a friend, how many times do you let the phone ring before you **hang up**?

7. Do you make your kids **hang up** their clothes?

8. When your friend is sad, how do you **cheer** him **up**?

9. Do you like your friends to **drop by**, or do you want them to call first?

10. Do you find job applications hard to **fill out**?

11. Can you **figure out** government forms?

12. Where did you **grow up**?

13. Do you **give up** easily, or do you **keep on** trying?

14. Have you ever played cards for money? If so, did you win, lose, or **break even**?

15. If things go badly at work, do you **take it out** on your family and friends?

Instructions

Hand out question slips to each student. Either hand the questions out one at a time or divide the question slips among the students at the beginning. Either way, have the students take turns asking each other questions.

WARNING!

It is vital the students know the two-part verbs (idioms) used in the questions before you play the game. It's a good idea to underline the idiom used in each question. I have used this activity as a review of two-part verbs both at the beginning of a class session and also as a "relaxer" at the end of a long class.

COUNT AND NON-COUNT GAMES

Students grasp the concept that there are things we can count and those we cannot. The problem lies in the English language which has different quantity words for things we count and don't count. For example, we use **much** with **milk**, but **many** with **glasses of milk**. After studying how to use **much, many, few, little, a few, a little,** and after doing exercises to strengthen learning, play games.

I did not use **a lot/a lot of** in this game, although their use certainly makes life simpler.

QUANTITY WORDS

High Beginning - Intermediate

Write sentences on slips of paper with blanks for the quantity word. On small slips of paper, write each quantity word.

1. When there is snow, there are _____ cars on the road.

2. Sorry, I can't help you now. I only have _____ minutes.

3. Only _____ rain falls in the desert.

4. Students often have _____ money to spend on extras.

5. People don't like him; therefore, he has _____ friends.

6. She drinks _____ pop everyday.

7. How _____ cans did she drink yesterday?

8. I always have _____ questions about English.

9. How _____ English do you know?

10. He has lived here only _____ months.

11. Too _____ TV isn't good for you. There are _____ programs I like to watch, only two or three.

12. How _____ beer can you drink?

13. On the news last night, there was _____ important news; it was mostly trivial.

14. I don't know why the police stopped me. I only had drunk _____ beers.

15. There is _____ information on the Internet, but only _____ is useful to me.

Hand out the sentence slips to each student. Create enough slips for each student to have at least four. Put quantity words in the middle of the table. Have students take turns reading their slips and selecting the correct quantity word. If the student is correct, s/he keeps the sentence slip. If not, s/he forfeits the slip and another student tries. Put quantity words back on the table after each student's turn. The winner is the student with the largest number of sentence slips.

Before students play this game, they must understand the difference between *few/little* and *a few/a little*. I tried this game with beginning students, and it was a big flop, because their command of English was too meager.

COUNT/NON-COUNT NOUNS PLUS PREPOSITIONS

Intermediate

Create a list of sentences for each student with blanks for count/non-count words and prepositions.

Put on the board much/many, not much/not many, a few, few, a little, little. Put on the board the prepositions possible: under, in front of, behind, next to, near, with, during, between, until, from, of, to, for, at, in, on.

1. _____ winter there is usually _____ snow in Alaska.

2. _____ my house there are _____ trees.

3. _____ I learn English, there are _____ jobs I can get.

4. _____ January and February there is _____ cold weather _____ the northern part _____ the United States.

5. I want _____ buy _____ things, but I don't have _____ money.

6. I don't need _____ sugar _____ my cake.

7. _____ the desert there is _____ water and _____ trees.

8. Q. How _____ words do you know _____ Spanish?
   A. Only _____.

9. _____ the states of the Northern Great Plains, there are _____ people.

10. When I go _____ work_____ the morning, there is _____ traffic.

11. _____ Boston and Washington, D.C., there are _____ large cities.

12. _____ Christmas there _____ sales _____ the stores.

13. Q. What are you going _____ do _____ Christmas day this year?
    A. Not _____. Just stay home and watch TV.

14. I'm very sad. I have _____ chance of getting a better job.

15. Why can't you hear me? You're standing right _____ me.

Tell the students how much time they have to complete the sentences. I allow at least fifteen minutes. At the end of the time allotted, have students take turns reading sentences. There are different possibilities for many of the sentences. This is a non-competitive game as only the student knows how many s/he gets right. I have asked if anyone got them all correct. None has so far.

GRAMMAR CHALLENGE

ONE DIE GAME

You can simplify this game by using only the present and future tenses. The game below uses some complex grammatical constructions. such as: "If I had had _____," or "He told me yesterday he _____ last week."

Intermediate-Advanced

You will need one die and sentence cards with one to six blank spaces on each card to correspond with the six sides of the die. Make at least five sentence cards for each set of blank spaces; that is, five cards with one blank, five with two blanks, etc. Number each sentence card with a 1, 2, 3, 4, 5, or 6.

Sample game:
1 blank: I enjoy _____.
             I don't want you to _____.
             Why do you always _____?
             He isn't _____.
             I'm confused about _____.

2 blanks: Riding a bicycle is _____ _____.
             We always _____ _____.
             What does _____ _____?
             We never _____ _____.
             She didn't _____ _____.

3 blanks: If you're sleepy, you _____ _____ _____.
             Did she forget _____ _____ _____?
             If you're hungry, you can _____ _____ _____.
             I'm thinking of _____ _____ _____.
             I'm interested in _____ _____ _____.

4 blanks: What does he usually _____ _____ _____ _____?
             In my family there are _____ _____ _____ _____.
             We went to _____ _____ _____ _____.
             If I had $1,000,000, _____ _____ _____ _____.
             He was sad because _____ _____ _____ _____.

5 blanks: In the fall we _____ _____ _____
             _____ _____.
             Does the plane _____ _____
             _____ _____ _____?
             I watched _____ _____ _____
             _____ _____.
             He complained about _____ _____
             _____ _____ _____.
             She insisted on_____ _____
             _____ _____ _____.

6 blanks: Have you ever _____ _____ _____
             _____ _____ _____?
             When I was a kid, _____ _____ _____
             _____ _____._____.
             In the evening, _____ _____
             _____ _____ _____ _____.
             What would you do if _____ _____
             _____ _____ _____?
             Next summer I _____ _____ _____
             _____ _____ _____.

Instructions   After a player rolls the die and, depending on the roll (1-6), s/he picks a corresponding numbered card and finishes the sentence orally with the

45

appropriate number of words. If the sentence makes sense, the student keeps the card.

The teacher, with the help of the other students, is the judge as to the acceptability of the sentence. This is not a fast paced game, because the student needs time to think about how to complete the sentence.

An alternative way to play the game is to have each student roll the die five times and pick the appropriate cards at the beginning of the game. Then all students could study their cards at the same time and think about how to complete the sentences. I've never done this, but it might speed up the game.

Variation:
If there are enough students, make two teams. Ask each team to throw the die for the other team. The members of each team help each other finish the sentence with the correct number of words.

You can see that to play this game students must know how to use different tenses, how to complete *if* conditional sentences, and what form of the verb to use after prepositions.

FAMILY RELATIONSHIPS GAMES

RELATIONSHIP DEFINITIONS

Intermediate-Advanced

Families are very important to the new immigrant. The purpose of the following game is to teach the English words for the relationships the student already knows in his own language.

Create small cards with names of relationships and cards with their definitions.

Relationship	Definition
brother	my mother's son
stepson	my wife's son, not my son
niece	my brother's daughter
nephew	my sister's son
uncle	my mother's brother
aunt	my uncle's wife

46

daughter-in-law	my son's wife
son-in-law	my daughter's husband
cousins	children of my aunt and uncle
wife	my children's mother
stepmother	my father's second wife
father	my grandmother's son
mother-in-law	my husband's mother
brother-in-law	my sister's husband
sister	my father's daughter
grandfather	my mother's father
great-grandmother	my father's mother's mother

Instructions

Spread out all definition cards face up on the table, put relationship cards face down in a pile. Have students take turns drawing a relationship card and matching it with the correct definition card. If s/he is correct, s/he keeps the cards. If not, the cards are put back on the table and in the pile, and another student takes a turn.

Variation for very advanced students:
Put all the relationships on the board. Then you or a student give the definition orally and have the rest guess the relationship. Cross out each relationship as it is correctly identified. This is a group activity rather than a competitive game.

DRIVER'S MANUAL GAMES

PREPARING FOR THE WRITTEN TEST

To a newly arrived immigrant, getting a driver's license is equivalent to getting a green card or a job; they all rank number one. In our school we work with students as a group or individually, when possible, to help them pass the written exam. If students can take the written test in their own languages, there is little need to play games. In my state, immigrants may take the test in one of three languages. If the language a immigrant speaks is not one of the three, s/he is on his own in English.

The following game is not exhaustive but can be used after the students have studied the manual for a while. The purpose is to underscore how much the student has learned and to encourage further learning.

DEFINITIONS OR SYNONYMS GAME

Preparation

Create two sets of cards written in different colored ink.

Cards to spread out	Cards in a pile
acceleration lane	entrance ramp
stop	red light
suspend	take away your license for a while
warning	yellow light
direction lights	turn signals
require	must
driving under the influence	D.U.I.
oncoming	approaching
slippery	slide easily
illegal	unlawful
depresses	slows down
allowed	permitted
hydrant	where fire engines can get water
accelerate	speed up
proceed with caution	go ahead carefully
decelerate	slow down
stalled car	a vehicle that cannot move
flammable vehicle	gasoline truck
pavement	hard surface road
towing	pulling a trailer or vehicle
flashing red light	stop, then go
dim	lower your lights
hazardous	dangerous

Instructions

Spread out one set of cards face up on the table; put the other set face down. Students take turns drawing and matching. They keep the correct pairs. The winner is the one with the largest number of correct pairs.

WARNING!

Advise your students that the words used in the manual are not always the same words used in the actual test. For example, in my state's manual regarding railroad crossings, it states, "These vehicles must stop within 50 feet." But on the test, the words "are required to stop" are used. I don't think that approaching and oncoming are synonyms, but in the driver's manual in my state, they are used interchangeably. Check the manual in your state.

Draw a map on a large poster board that shows:
>   Special two-way left turn lanes.
>   Intersections of two-lane streets.
>   Intersections of four-lane streets.
>   Intersections of two and four-lane streets.

To turn left from a One Way to a One Way, begin turn from Left Lane and turn into Left Lane.	To turn left from a Two Way road to a One Way road, begin the turn with Left wheels close to center line of road and enter the Left Lane of the One Way road.	To turn left from a Two Way road onto a four lane highway, approach the turn with left wheels close to centerline of road. Make the turn and enter left lane of four-lane highway.	Two Way Left Turn Lane

Make small traffic signs from stick-em notes to use on the map, such as: *Stop, Yield, One Way, No U Turn, Stop Light, Do Not Enter*. I also draw a tree and lamp post on stick-em notes to help with the section on judging following distances.

I use a poster board with four different layouts, using stick-em notes, can create a variety of realistic traffic situations. You will also need a few toy cars and trucks. Have this teaching tool on hand while you and the students are going through the driver's manual and before s/he takes the behind-the-wheel test.

Notes

Your best and most enthusiastic teachers will be those who have already passed the test and want to help their fellow students.

WORD GAMES

The following games play around with words. They range from fairly simple to complex. The students I have worked with love to try out their knowledge of the English language and prove they can understand and manipulate it.

WHICH WORD IS DIFFERENT AND WHY?

High Beginning - Intermediate

Create a sheet of paper with a list of words used in the game for each student. Game One Sample:

1. blanket	towel	pillow	sheets
2. sun	rain	snow	sleet
3. occasionaly	sometimes	now and then	always
4. newspaper	TV	book	magazine
5. owner	tenant	renter	lodger
6. sitting	kneeling	standing	crouching
7. beer	coffee	water	milk
8. bowl	plate	cup	glass
9. opinion	idea	fact	thought
10. steal	borrow	lend	loan

Answer explanations
1. TOWEL not used on a bed.
2. SUN doesn't fall from the sky.
3. ALWAYS is not temporary.
4. TV not read.
5. OWNER doesn't pay rent.
6. STANDING - others have bended knees.
7. BEER is alcoholic.
8. A PLATE you put food on; with others, you put food in.
9. FACT. Others are personal ideas.
10. STEAL. Others are legal transactions.

The object of the game is to decide which of the four words in each line is different from the others and to tell why it is different. Students will come up with other reasons why a word is different. Any logical reason is acceptable. Before you begin to play, make sure the students understand all words in the series.

First allow ten to fifteen minutes for students to work by themselves. Then have students take turns reading their answers and giving reasons for their choices. These games are noncompetitive; no winners and no losers.

WHAT DO THE WORDS HAVE IN COMMON?

Student Preparation

High Beginning - Intermediate

Create a sheet of paper with a list of game words for each student. Sample:

1. elephant	mountain	skyscraper	Statue of Liberty
2. typewriter	book	a letter	the alphabet
3. cotton candy	snow	baby's skin	pillow
4. cabbage	address	sweater	lettuce
5. pencil	desk	tree	matches
6. rabbit	racing car	jet	spaceship
7. snowball	ice cube	winter	freezer
8. mirror	window	light bulb	TV screen
9. typewriter	car	computer	door
10. turtle	learning English	very old car	coming of spring

Answer explanations

1. All big	6. All fast
2. All have letters	7. All cold
3. All soft	8. All made of glass
4. All have 7 letters	9. All have a key
5. All made of wood	10. All very slow

The object of the game is to decide what the four words in each line have in common and to tell why.

Intermediate

Create a sheet of paper with a list of words used in the game for each student. There may well be more than one answer.

1. socks	sweater	shoes	jeans
2. car	bicycle	raft	canoe
3. girl	TV	needle	potato
4. tomorrow	necessary	wonderful	notebook
5. three	seven	nine	two
6. lights	computer	window	car
7. clock	a watch	brake	speedometer
8. toes	thigh	fingers	ankle
9. cabbage	lettuce	radishes	peas
10. walk	run	sit	jump
11. beets	carrots	onions	lettuce
12. car	airplane	bicycle	bus
13. boy	kitten	radio	tree
14. matches	pencil	board	nail
15. pens	pants	scissors	shoes

Answer explanations
1. SWEATER you put over your head.
2. CAR has a motor.
3. TV doesn't have eyes.
4. WONDERFUL doesn't have double letters.
5. TWO is an even number.
6. WINDOW - you don't turn on.

7. BRAKE doesn't have a dial.
8. FINGERS - others part of the leg.
9. RADISHES - all others are green.
10. SIT. All others are action verbs.
11. LETTUCE. Others are root vegetables.
12. CAR. Get in rather than get on.
13. RADIO. All others grow.
14. NAIL. Others made of wood.
15. PENS. Others are all a pair of.

Instructions

The object of the game is to decide which of the four words in each line is different from the others and to tell why it is different.

Notes

Other possibilities are below. I never use more than fifteen sets of words in one game.

cheese	cream	butter	margarine
(MARGARINE not made of milk.)			
tornado	hurricane	tsunami	typhoon
(TORNADO is on land.)			
window	eyeglasses	mirror	windshield
(MIRROR. Can't see through.)			
photograph	map	recipe	dictionary
(PHOTOGRAPH. You don't read.)			
Oregon	California	Colorado	Washington
(COLORADO. Not on an ocean.)			

HOW SIMILAR? HOW DIFFERENT?

Student

Intermediate - Advanced

Preparation

The rules and the materials needed are the same as for the previous games. Any logical reason for sameness or difference should be encouraged and applauded.

Sample game:
The words in the following sets have something in common. In each set there is also one word that is different. Ask students to decide what each set has in common and which word is different. Why?

1. car	shopping cart	bicycle	roller blades

2.	gas meter	recipe	magazine	newspaper
3.	airplane	taxi	bus	horse
4.	red	navy blue	purple	pink
5.	gas	milk	pop	water
6.	scissors	pants	socks	sunglasses
7.	elbow	knee	back	ankle
8.	Saturday	Monday	Tuesday	Thursday
9.	man	woman	boy	child
10.	jump	smile	run	walk
11.	river	creek	ocean	lake
12.	Yield	Slippery when wet	Stop	No U Turn
13.	gold	silver	oil	coal
14.	airplane seat	couch	rocking chair	armchair
15.	star	moon	planet	sun

Answer explanations
1. All have wheels. Shopping cart used inside.
2. All are read. Gas meter has numbers, not letters.
3. All means of transportation. Taxi • get in, not on.
4. All colors. Pink is a light color.
5. All liquids. Gas you don't drink.
6. All pairs. You don't wear scissors.
7. All parts of the body. Back is not a joint.
8. All days of the week. Monday has no s. in it.
9. All people. Boy has a regular plural.
10. All verbs. Smile you don't use your feet.
11. All water. Ocean is salty.
12. All traffic signs. Slippery when wet only warning sign.
13. All in the ground. Oil is not mined.

14. All "sittable." Sit on a couch, sit in the others.
15. All in the sky. Sun you see only in the day.

It is vital that students have a chance to look over all the words in a series to be sure they understand each word. And be sure to allow enough time for students to ask questions before you play any of the preceding games.

WHAT'S THE WORD?

We've had lots of fun with these games. They're challenging and frustrating. You will need a good thesaurus on hand for students to use. Roget's Thesaurus and Webster's Thesaurus are two good resources.

Student

Preparation

Advanced

The following two games involve pairs of words that begin and end with the same letter. Each word in a pair has the same number of letters. There are also definitions and parts of speech given. The answers, for your benefit, are at the extreme right.

Create a list for each student with definitions, words with correct number of blank spaces, and parts of speech.

GAME ONE

Definitions	Words	Part of Speech	Answer
1. It means very odd.	w _ _ _ d	adjective	weird
2. It means all the countries on earth.	w _ _ _ d	noun	world
3. It means to wait, hope for.	e _ _ _ _ t	verb	expect
4. It means all others but.	e _ _ _ _ t	preposition	except
5. It means to feel alone and sad.	l _ _ _ _ y	adjective	lonely
6. It means someone or something nice.	l _ _ _ _ y	adjective	lovely

7. It means a narrow passage-way in a store or theater.	a_ _ _e	noun	aisle
8. It means no one is with you.	a_ _ _e	adverb, adjective	alone
9. It means later.	a_ _ _r	preposition	after
10. It means to change.	a_ _ _r	verb	alter
11. It means glad.	h_ _ _y	adjective	happy
12. It means it weighs a lot.	h_ _ _y	adjective	heavy
13. It means similar.	a_ _ _e	adjective	alike
14. It means to think the same as another person.	a_ _ _e	verb	agree

Instructions

Allow fifteen or twenty minutes for each of the following seven word games. Students may work individually or team up with another student. At the end of the allotted time, have the students take turns reading their words out loud. The student or team with the greatest number of correct words wins the game.

Notes

My advanced students were very rarely able to complete the list of words.

GAME TWO

Preparation

Same as Game One.

Definitions	Words	Parts of Speech	Answer
1. It means probable, believable.	l_ _ _ _y	adjective/adverb	likely
2. It means full of life.	l_ _ _ _y	adjective/adverb	lively
3. It means to say some one has done something wrong.	a_ _ _ _e	verb	accuse
4. It means to recommend, to suggest.	a_ _ _ _e	verb	advise

5. It means to love very, very much.	a_ _ _e	verb	adore
6. It means to quarrel, to fight with words.	a_ _ _e	verb	argue
7. It means clumsy.	a_ _ _ _ _d	adjective	awkward
8. It means to respect, look up to, in the past.	a_ _ _ _ _d	adjective	admired
9. It means to plan or to put in order.	a_ _ _ _ _e	verb	arrange
10. It means the lack of someone/something.	a_ _ _ _ _e	noun	absence
11. It means the way you feel or think about something/someone.	a_ _ _ _ _ _e	noun	attitude
12. It means people who watch or listen, as at a play or concert.	a_ _ _ _ _ _e	noun	audience
13. It means before in time, not now.	f_ _ _ _ _ _y	adverb	formerly
14. It means in a polite and proper way.	f_ _ _ _ _ _y	adverb	formally

GAME THREE

This game also works with pairs of words that have the same number of letters in each pair of words and begin and end with the same letter, but the format is different; the words are longer and more difficult. However, I have found that a word like *prejudice* is often times more understandable than a word like *while*. As in the previous games a good thesaurus or dictionary is necessary to prevent extreme frustration. The answers are for your benefit.

Create a list for each student with blanks for each missing letter and the definition.

1. l _ _ _ _ _ e   what you must have before you drive.

2. l _ _ _ _ _ e   an informational talk, often given by a teacher in a class.

3. p _ _ _ _ _ _ _ _ _ n means sweat.

4. p _ _ _ _ _ _ _ _ _ n what the doctor gives to take to the drugstore.

5. l _ _ _ _ _ y   another word for freedom.

6. l _ _ _ _ _ y   a place for many books.

7. p _ _ _ _ _ _ y   it may or can happen.

8. p _ _ _ _ _ _ y   it's likely to happen.

9. w _ _ _ e   the largest mammal in the sea.

10. w _ _ _ e   during a period of time.

11. p _ _ _ _ _ _ e   to get ready to do something.

12. p _ _ _ _ _ _ e   is an area, flat with very few trees.

13. s _ _ _ _ _ r   is a small plate to put a cup on.

14. s _ _ _ _ _ r   what most countries call football.

15. s _ _ _ _ _ _ _ _ y   what you write letters on.

16. s _ _ _ _ _ _ _ _ y   what you cannot move.

17. p _ _ _ _ _ _ _ e   is a bias.

18. p _ _ _ _ _ _ _ e   is a right to do something.

19. p _ _ _ _ _ _ _ _ n   is a very unusual happening.

20. p _ _ _ _ _ _ _ _ n   trying to get someone to do what you want.

21. e _ _ _ _ _ _ y   is a plea.

22. e _ _ _ _ _ _ y   means completely.

23. e _ _ _ _ _ _ t   is to give something to someone else for protection.

24. e _ _ _ _ _ t   is to delight, charm.

Answers

1. license	9. whale	17. prejudice
2. lecture	10. while	18. privilege
3. perspiration	11. prepare	19. phenomenon
4. prescription	12. prairie	20. persuasion
5. liberty	13. saucer	21. entreaty
6. library	14. soccer	22. entirely
7. possibly	15. stationery	23. entrust
8. probably	16. stationary	24. enchant

Instructions

Allow at least twenty minutes to play. Have students play individually or in pairs. As in Games One and Two, the student or pair with the greatest number of correct words wins.

GAME FOUR

Student

Intermediate

Preparation

Create a list for each student with blank spaces and the definitions.

			Answers
1.	_ _ _ _	They're good to eat as dessert.	pies
2.	_ _ _ _	Saying things that are false.	lies
3.	_ _ _ _	You usually have three of these a day.	meal
4.	_ _ _ _	What a doctor tries to do.	heal
5.	_ _ _ _	What you do with Easter eggs.	hide
6.	_ _ _ _	What do you do with a bicycle.	ride
7.	_ _ _ _ _	Maybe.	might
8.	_ _ _ _ _	Opposite of wrong.	right
9.	_ _ _ _	Opposite of front.	rear
10.	_ _ _ _	What falls from your eye when you cry.	tear
11.	_ _ _ _ _ _	Prefer.	rather
12.	_ _ _ _ _ _	Result of using shaving cream.	lather
13.	_ _ _ _	Not cold, not hot.	warm
14.	_ _ _ _	Hurt someone, something.	harm

15. _ _ _ _	Not pass a test.	fail
16. _ _ _ _	What you do with a letter you write.	mail
17. _ _ _ _	At the back of your foot.	heel
18. _ _ _ _	What you do with an orange before you eat it.	peel
19. _ _ _ _ _ _	Quit a job.	resign
20. _ _ _ _ _ _	A pattern or a picture.	design
21. _ _ _ _ _	There are 24 of them in one day.	hours
22. _ _ _ _ _	Guided trips.	tours
23. _ _ _ _ _	What you put your food into.	mouth
24. _ _ _ _ _	One of the four directions.	south
25. _ _ _ _	Not all.	some
26. _ _ _ _	Where you live.	home

Instructions

Tell your students that ONLY the first letter of each word is different. They all have the same number of letters, and most of the words rhyme.

As in the previous games, students may play individually or in pairs. Allow at least fifteen minutes. The student or team with the greatest number of correct words wins.

GAMES FIVE - SEVEN

The answers to Games Five through Seven are at the end of this series. See how you do. The exercise will help you understand the frustration of your students. Use only one game per class session.

Student

High Intermediate and Advanced Students

I used these word games at the beginning of the class period in the advanced class. They usually led to questions and discussion as to usage and acceptability in various situations. Although frustrating at times, the students looked forward to the challenge.

Preparation

Provide a list for each student with the blanks and the sentences. Each game has a separate list.

There is only a one letter difference between each word, as in the previous games, but the clues are sentences rather than definitions and the one letter that is different may not be the first letter.

Instructions

The rules for playing and winning are the same as for the previous four games. Tell your students some words rhyme, others do not.

GAME FIVE

1. _ _ _ _ _ _   My _____ is 5'6".
2. _ _ _ _ _ _   My _____ is 125 lbs.

3. _ _ _ _   My favorite _____ is lamb.
4. _ _ _ _   Small boys wear out the knees and the _____ of their jeans first.

5. _ _ _ _   Please stand behind the white _____.
6. _ _ _ _   That's not yours. It's _____.

7. _ _ _ _   Don't _____ at me that way!
8. _ _ _ _   Who _____ my wallet?

9. _ _ _ _   You sing very well. May I _____ your voice?
10. _ _ _ _   I can use a computer, but not a _____ writer.

11. _ _ _ _   Do you like _____ games?
12. _ _ _ _   Learning a new language is _____.

13. _ _ _ _   Sometimes when I do the laundry, I lose a _____.
14. _ _ _ _   Don't forget to _____ the door when you leave.

15. _ _ _ _   Don't _____ me in the ribs with your elbow.
16. _ _ _ _   A _____ makes me laugh.

17. _ _ _ _ _   He always _____ for his girlfriend to finish getting ready to go out on a date.
18. _ _ _ _ _   That light bulb has 100 _____.

19. _ _ _ _   This winter, we have had too much _____.
20. _ _ _ _   I hate to get behind a _____ driver.

GAME SIX

1. _ _ _ _   What's your _____?
2. _ _ _ _   Would you like to play a _____?

3. _ _ _ _   I hit him in the face with my _____.
4. _ _ _ _   It's not raining, but there's a _____ falling.

5. _ _ _ _   Would you like some _____ coffee?
6. _ _ _ _   She _____ purple shoes, pink pants, and a red sweater. Ufta!

7. _ _ _ _   Some people always have good _____.
8. _ _ _ _   Most Americans want to make a fast _____ and get rich quick.

9. _ _ _ _ _   Shopping _____ have replaced downtown stores in most cities.
10. _ _ _ _ _   _____ are supposed to be more aggressive than females.

11. _ _ _ _ _   My daughter dressed up as a _____ on Halloween.
12. _ _ _ _ _   _____ one do you want?

13. _ _ _ _ _ _   Australia is a huge _____.
14. _ _ _ _ _ _   California is on the coast; North Dakota is _____.

15. _ _ _ _ _ _   You have very good eye _____.
16. _ _ _ _ _   A slang word for <u>drunk</u> is _____.

17. _ _ _ _ _ _ _ _   He _____ her when he told her he loved her, because he really didn't.
18. _ _ _ _ _ _ _ _   Have you _____ a letter from your parents recently?

19. _ _ _ _ _ _   My sister just had a baby girl. I have a new _____.
20. _ _ _ _ _   I'd like another _____ of pie, please.

21. _ _ _ _ _ _   We had to sign a _____ for our apartment.
22. _ _ _ _ _   I like people to _____ me, but not make fun of me.

GAME SEVEN

1. _ _ _ _ _   Lemons _____ sour.
2. _ _ _ _ _   If you don't want it, just throw it in the _____ basket.

3. _ _ _ _   Her husband robbed a store and went to _____ .
4. _ _ _ _   She put up $10,000 _____ to get him out.

5. _ _ _ _   I crawled under a barbed-wire fence and now my jeans are _____.
6. _ _ _ _   I've worked hard all day and now I'm all _____-out.

7. _ _ _ _ _   I'm too short. I can't _____ it.
8. _ _ _ _ _   Most people _____ negatively when they're criticized.

9. _ _ _ _ _ _ _   Help! Call a _____. The water pipe is broken.
10. _ _ _ _ _ _ _   _____ is another word for sleep.

11. _ _ _ _ _   You'll need a _____ to explore that river.
12. _ _ _ _ _   I like to watch skaters _____ across the ice.

13. _ _ _ _ _   The color of most _____ is white.
14. _ _ _ _ _   _____ candles are long and slim; votive candles are short and stubby.

15. _ _ _ _ _   Kids like to play a staring game to see who will ____ first.
16. _ _ _ _ _   I couldn't think of the answer. My mind just went _____.

17. _ _ _ _ _ _ _   She went to the _____ for the new drama. She hopes to get a starring role.
18. _ _ _ _ _ _ _   Kids in grade school learn _____ before they learn subtraction.

19. _ _ _   Before you leave on your trip, you'd better get a good _____.

20. _ _ _   My cat sat on my _____ and purred.

21. _ _ _ _   I'd rather eat with a spoon than a _____.
22. _ _ _ _   I'd rather listen to _____ music than country-western.

ANSWERS TO WORD GAMES FIVE - SEVEN

The answer keys below are for the preceding three games and include notes about problems we had in playing the games. Our problems may not be your problems. But you know if you see a blank look on a student's face, you have a problem to deal with.

GAME FIVE

1. height	6. mine	11. card	16. joke
2. weight	7. look	12. hard	17. waits
3. meat	8. took	13. sock	18. watts
4. seat	9. tape	14. lock	19. snow
5. line	10. type	15. poke	20. slow

Notes

For #14, students may guess *shut* or *close*. Ask for a word that means to make a house safe. For #18, students may not know *watts* is a word.

GAME SIX

1. name	7. luck	13. island	19. niece
2. game	8. buck	14. inland	20. piece
3. fist	9. malls	15. sight	21. lease
4. mist	10. males	16. tight	22. tease
5. more	11. witch	17. deceived	
6. wore	12. which	18. received	

Notes

For #8, *buck* is a slang word they should know. For #14, inland was a new word for my students. For #16, *tight* is a slang word that may be new to your students. For #17, *deceived* will be new, but after *received*, tell them the first letter for #17 is different.

GAME SEVEN

1. taste	7. reach	13. paper	19. map
2. waste	8. react	14. taper	20. lap
3. jail	9. plumber	15. blink	21. fork
4. bail	10. slumber	16. blank	22. folk
5. torn	11. guide	17. audition	
6. worn	12. glide	18. addition	

Most students know *prison* not *jail* (3), and are totally unfamiliar with *bail* (4). Students know *plumber* (10). Tell them the first letter in #10 is different. G*uide* (11) was new to my students. Tell students to look up other words for *slide, skate* (12). Paper was easy, but taper was unknown to my students (13, 14). Surprisingly, they knew *audition* (17).

GENERAL KNOWLEDGE GAMES

Q & A

High Beginning

Write two sets of cards, one set for the questions and one set for the answers. Write each set with a different colored marker.

Sample game:
1. How many days are there in one year?

2. How much is 9 x 9?

3. What are the four seasons of the year?

4. Who arrived in America in 1492?

5. How much is 24 + 24?

6. How many states are there in the United States?

7. What is the capital of the United States?

8. What days are the weekend?

9. When is Independence Day in the United States?

10. 0 degrees Celsius is how many degrees Fahrenheit?

11. What is the largest state in the U.S.?

12. What is the smallest state in the U.S.?

13. What is the world's most spoken language?

14. What is the second most spoken language in the world?

15. What state in the U.S. has the most rainfall?

16. What is the most popular drink in the U.S.?

17. In what month is the shortest day of the year?

18. In what month is the longest day of the year?

19. How many players are there on a soccer (football) team?

20. How many time zones are there in the continental U.S.?

1. 365	11. Alaska
2. 81	12. Rhode Island
3. Winter, spring, summer, fall	13. Chinese
4. Columbus	14. English
5. 48	15. Hawaii
6. 50	16. Milk
7. Washington D.C.	17. December
8. Saturday and Sunday	18. June
9. July 4th	19. 11
10. 32	20. 4

Instructions

To play the game, spread out all answer cards face up and put the question cards face down in a pile. Students take turns drawing a question card and finding the answer card on the table. If a student finds the correct answer, he keeps the two cards. If the answer is not correct, it goes back on the table. The student who has the most questions answered correctly wins.

PAIRING PHRASES

GAME ONE

Student

Intermediate

Preparation

Write two sets of cards with different colored markers, one color for the beginning phrase (black) and another with the ending phrase (green).

Sample phrases:
1. My father's mother is my **grandmother**.

2. The name of our country's song is **the Star-Spangled Banner.**

3. The two largest political parties in the U.S. are **Republican and Democrat.**

4. Abraham Lincoln was **assassinated.**

5. Japan **has the most earthquakes.**

6. A revolutionary war is **when one country fights to be free from another country.**

7. George Washington is the **father of our country.**

8. The daughter of my brother is my **niece.**

9. Before 1863 Alaska was called **Russian America.**

10. The son of my sister is my **nephew.**

11 . A woman who puts on lipstick and eyeshadow wears **makeup.**

12. A civil war is **when people of the same country fight each other.**

13. The largest city in China is **Shanghai.**

14. The founder of Islam is **Mohammed.**

15. The financial capital of the U.S. is **New York.**

Instructions

To play the game, lay out the sets of cards with beginning and ending phrases face up, OR lay out the ending phrase cards face up and put the other set face down in a pile for students to draw from. Either way, the students take turns matching the correct beginning and ending phrases. The student with the most cards wins.

Notes

I have found that these game(s) go more smoothly if there are two sets of cards for each five students. Therefore, if your class is large enough for team play, have the students on each team work together. The team with the most cards wins.

GAME TWO

Intermediate-Advanced

Write two sets of cards with different colored markers, one color for the beginning phrase (black) and another with the ending phrase (green).

Sample phrases:
1. Water boils at **212 degrees Fahrenheit.**

2. In a circle there are **360 degrees.**

3. The most Americans died in the **Civil War.**

4. The number of continents in the world is **seven.**

5. In some countries, water faucets are **red and blue.**

6. The name of Ho Chi Minh city before 1975 was **Saigon.**

7. Football is played on a field that is a **rectangle.**

8. The first country to try to build a canal across Panama was **France.**

9. If it's 4:00 p.m. in Denver, in Washington, D.C. it's **6:00 p.m.**

10. If it's 4:00 p.m. in New York, in Seattle it's **1:00 p.m.**

11. Normal body temperature (Fahrenheit) is **98.6 degrees.**

12. The tallest grass in the world is **bamboo.**

13. The highest place in the world is **Mr. Everest.**

14. The saltiest sea in the world is the **Dead Sea.**

15. The United States won its independence in the **Revolutionary War.**

16. The second largest state in the U.S. is **Texas.**

17. The number of ounces in a pound is **16.**

18. The number of teaspoons in a tablespoon is **3.**

19. In the U.S. the unlucky number is **13.**

20. The number of planets in our solar system is **8.**

Instructions To play the game, lay out the sets of cards with beginning and ending phrases face up, OR lay out the ending phrase cards face up and put the other set face down in a pile for students to draw from. Either way, the students take turns matching the correct beginning and ending phrases. The student with the most cards wins.

GAME THREE

Student

High Intermediate-Advanced

Preparation Write two sets of cards with different colored markers, one color for the beginning phrase (black) and another with the ending phrase (green).

Sample phrases:
1. The longest river in the U.S. is the **Mississippi River.**

2. Montana is the source of the **Missouri River.**

3. A metropolitan area has many **suburbs.**

4. Three states in New England are **Connecticut, Vermont, and Rhode Island.**

5. Three states in the South are **Alabama, Georgia, and Mississippi.**

6. Three states in the Mid-West are **Iowa, Illinois, and Minnesota.**

7. Three states in the West are **Colorado, Oregon, and Utah.**

8. The continental United States does NOT include **Alaska and Hawaii.**

9. Wheat, cotton, and corn are **crops.**

10. Coal, water, oil, and wood are **natural resources.**

11. The state with the most people is **California.**

12. A deep valley with steep sides is a **canyon.**

13. The mouth of the Mississippi River is at the **Gulf of Mexico.**

14. The source of the Mississippi River is in **Minnesota.**

15. The largest city in the Mid-West is **Chicago.**

16. The capital of Afghanistan is **Kabul.**

17. The capital of Turkey is **Ankara.**

18. The capital of Egypt is **Cairo.**

19. The capital of Ukraine is **Kiev.**

20. The longest river in the world is the **Nile.**

Instructions

To play the game, lay out the sets of cards with beginning and ending phrases face up, OR lay out the ending phrase cards face up and put the other set face down in a pile for students to draw from. Either way, the students take turns matching the correct beginning and ending phrases. The student with the most cards wins.

WARNING!

For any of the four previous games, it is most important that the students have a chance to ask questions about any words that might be unfamiliar to them.

Notes

These games may be played as pre-class activities (noncompetitive) as well as in-class or end-of-class competitive games. One of my volunteer teachers used very successfully the Intermediate -- Advanced general knowledge games as pre-class activities.

INDEX

www.ingramcontent.com/pod-product-compliance
Lightning Source LLC
Chambersburg PA
CBHW042008080426
42733CB00004B/43

9780615677439